Living Things
and Their Habitats

Welcome to the Coral Reef

by Honor Head

Ruby Tuesday Books

Published in 2017 by Ruby Tuesday Books Ltd.

Editor: Jean Coppendale
Designer: Emma Randall
Consultant: Sally Morgan
Production: John Lingham

Photo credits
Alamy: 6, 7 (top), 11 (bottom), 12 (top), 18, 23 (top); FLPA: 8 (top), 16 (top), 17, 19 (bottom), 20 (bottom), 21 (bottom), 25, 27, 29; Getty Images: 9; Istock Photo: 13; Shutterstock: Cover, 2–3, 4–5, 7 (main), 8 (bottom), 10, 11 (top), 12 (bottom), 14–15, 16 (bottom), 19 (top), 20 (top), 21 (top), 22, 23 (bottom), 24, 26, 28, 30–31.

British Library Cataloguing in Publication Data (CIP) is available for this title.

ISBN 978-1-911341-52-9

Printed in China by Toppan Leefung

www.rubytuesdaybooks.com

Contents

Words shown in **bold** in the text
are explained in the glossary.

Welcome to a Coral Reef

Who and what lives on the Great Barrier Reef?

This vast **coral reef** is home to plants, fish, sea anemones and turtles.

The plants and animals get what they need to live from their **habitat**.

A coral reef is a type of ecosystem. An ecosystem includes all the living things in an area. It also includes non-living things, such as the sun and sea. Everything in an ecosystem has its own part to play.

The Great Barrier Reef is in the Coral Sea off the coast of Australia.

Let's find out what happens in this habitat. Welcome to a coral reef!

What Is a Coral Reef?

A coral reef is built by tiny animals called coral polyps.

Some types of coral polyps have a hard, rock-like, outer skeleton.

Polyp

Skeleton

A reef starts to form when a coral polyp attaches itself to a rock on the sea floor.

The single coral begins to bud, or divide itself in half, to make another coral.

Billions of corals join together to form a single colony, or group.

A coral colony

Many colonies join up on the sea floor to form a rocky coral reef.

The Great Barrier Reef has formed throughout an area as big as 48 million football pitches!

A section of the Great Barrier Reef

Coral reef

What do corals feed on?

Invisible World

The sea is home to tiny animals and plants called **plankton**.

Plankton can only be seen under a microscope.

A coral polyp

Tentacles

Plankton also includes living things called **algae**.

Some coral polyps use their stinging **tentacles** to catch plankton to eat.

Some algae live inside the bodies of corals.

The algae use sunlight to make food for energy.

The corals also get energy from the food that's made by the algae.

Tentacles

Coral polyp

Zooxanthellae algae

The algae that live inside corals are called zooxanthellae (ZOH-oh-ZAN-thell-ee). In return for giving the corals food, the algae get a place to live where they are safe from animals.

Why is sunshine very important to the coral reef?

9

Sunlight for Survival

Sunlight is very important to a coral reef.

This is because algae need plenty of sunlight to make food for themselves and the coral.

To be healthy, a coral reef also needs the ocean to stay at just the right temperature. If the water gets too hot or too cold this can kill the algae, and the coral dies.

Over thousands of years, corals form and the reef grows and spreads.

A sea slug crawling over coral

A moray eel hides in coral, waiting to catch fish.

When a coral dies, its hard skeleton is left behind and becomes part of the rocky reef.

In time, the reef becomes like a busy underwater city that's home to millions of different animals.

What coral reef creatures look like plants but are actually animals?

Soft Corals and Sea Anemones

Some corals do not have a hard skeleton and do not build reefs.

These are called soft corals.

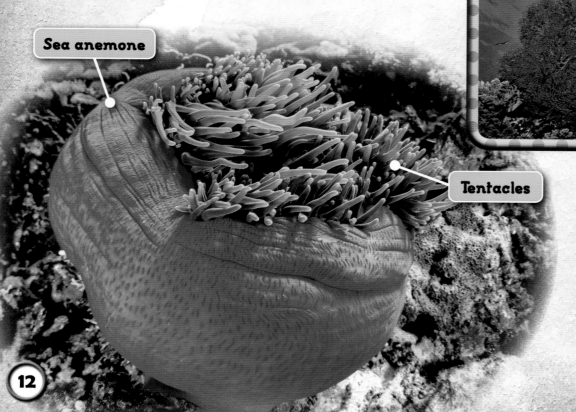

Soft coral

Sea anemone

Tentacles

Soft corals often look like plants, but they are animals.

Sea anemones also look like plants but are actually animals.

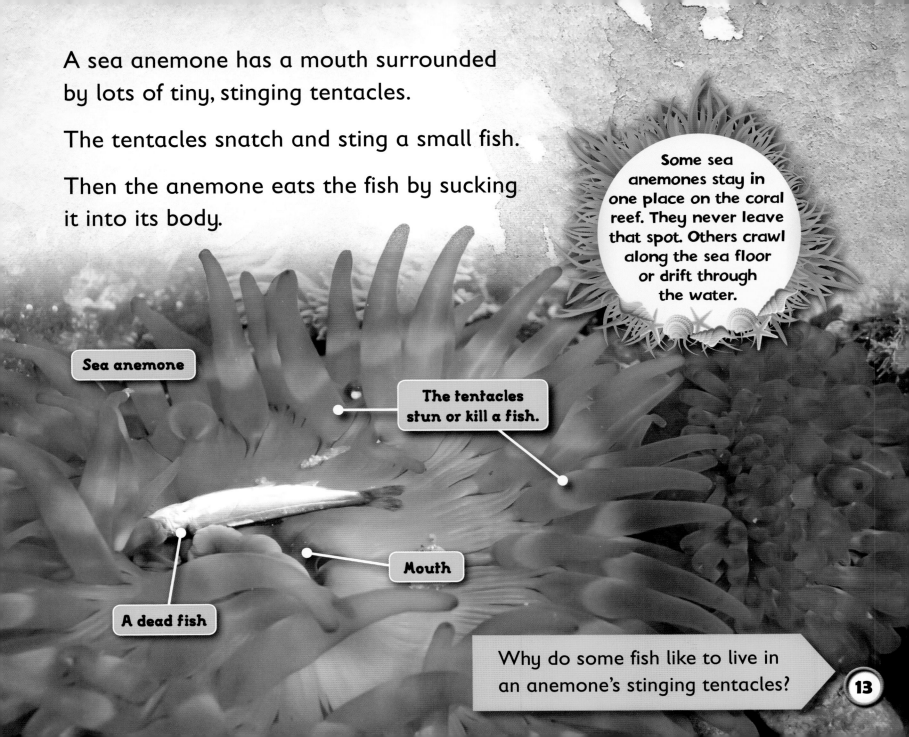

A sea anemone has a mouth surrounded by lots of tiny, stinging tentacles.

The tentacles snatch and sting a small fish.

Then the anemone eats the fish by sucking it into its body.

Some sea anemones stay in one place on the coral reef. They never leave that spot. Others crawl along the sea floor or drift through the water.

Sea anemone

The tentacles stun or kill a fish.

Mouth

A dead fish

Why do some fish like to live in an anemone's stinging tentacles?

A Special Partnership

Tiny clownfish live close to sea anemones.

The clownfish are tasty food for bigger fish and other reef **predators**.

Clownfish

If a clownfish is threatened, it swims among an anemone's tentacles.

Sea anemone

The stinging tentacles keep the clownfish safe from its predator.

The clownfish is covered with a slimy **mucus** that protects it from the anemone's stings.

In return for protection, a clownfish keeps the anemone clean. It nibbles bits of leftover food from the anemone's tentacles. This cleaning helps to keep the anemone healthy.

What animal is laying her eggs in a coral reef hideaway?

All Change

A cuttlefish is hunting for worms, shrimps, crabs and fish on the coral reef.

She can change her skin colour, pattern and **texture** in seconds.

Cuttlefish

Camouflaged cuttlefish

This **camouflage** helps her hide from predators.

The cuttlefish lays her eggs and hides them from predators in the rocky reef.

The baby cuttlefish usually hatch about two months later.

Cuttlefish eggs

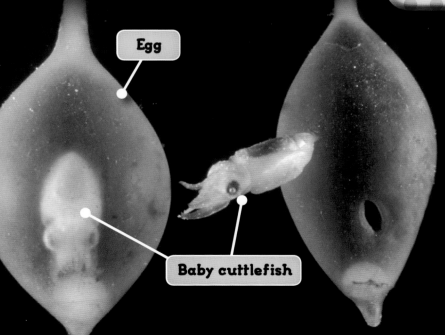

Egg

Baby cuttlefish

Baby cuttlefish feed on tiny crabs, shrimp and plankton.

The coral reef is very busy. What has arrived for a clean?

At the Cleaning Station

Large fish called manta rays visit the coral reef for a very special reason.

They line up at places called cleaning stations to be cleaned — by fish!

Manta ray

Sharks and other fish also enjoy a good clean at the cleaning stations.

Cleaner fish nibble away dead skin and **parasites** on a ray's body.

They even clean inside the ray's mouth and **gills**.

The fish get a meal, and their cleaning work helps keep the manta ray healthy.

Manta ray

Mouth

Cleaner fish

Gills

A giant moray eel having its mouth cleaned.

Why is the coral reef important for birds?

Bird Stops

In some parts of the Great Barrier Reef sand has built up on the coral and formed islands.

Island

Coral reef

Trees and other plants grow on the islands.

Thousands of birds visit the forest islands to **mate** and raise their chicks.

Noddy birds meeting up to mate.

A red-tailed tropicbird lays one egg on the ground under a tree.

Red-tailed tropicbird

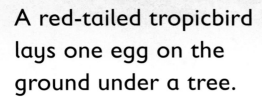

The forests are a safe place for the birds. The trees give them shelter from the hot sun and there are very few predators here.

Chick

When her chick hatches, the ocean around the reef provides plenty of fish to feed the baby bird.

What other animals come to the coral reef islands to lay their eggs?

Turtle Nursery

Green sea turtles come to Raine Island on the Great Barrier Reef to lay their eggs.

A female green sea turtle

Flipper

Turtle eggs

A turtle digs a hole in the sandy beach with her flippers.

She lays her eggs in the hole and covers them with sand.

Then the turtle goes back to her life in the sea.

The baby turtles hatch from their eggs under the sand. They can take two days to push themselves out of the sand.

A baby turtle climbing from its nest hole.

When the baby turtles hatch, they must make a dangerous journey to the sea.

As they crawl to the water, birds try to catch and eat them.

What plant is growing in an underwater meadow?

Seagrass Meadows

Meadows of seagrass grow in shallow water around the coral reef.

Green sea turtle

Seagrass

A dugong is also known as a sea cow.

Seagrass is an important food for turtles, dugongs and fish.

A leafy seadragon is hard to see in the seagrass.

It looks like seaweed floating in the water.

This camouflage helps it to stay safe from predators.

Leafy seadragon

Many fish lay their eggs in the seagrass meadows. The grasses are a safe place for baby fish to grow before they swim out to sea.

What visitors swim thousands of miles to mate and raise babies at the reef?

A Safe Place for Baby Whales

Huge humpback whales travel thousands of miles from freezing-cold Antarctica to the Great Barrier Reef.

The whales mate at the reef and then swim back to Antarctica.

The next year, the females return to the reef to give birth.

Whale calves have very little body fat so they would not survive in the icy waters of Antarctica.

Humpback whale

A mother whale feeds her calf plenty of rich milk so it can build up its body fat. After a few months, when the baby has grown, they make the long journey back to Antarctica.

At the reef the water is warm.

There are fewer large sharks and other predators that might attack a calf.

Mother whale

Calf

When is a whale not a whale?

When Is a Whale Not a Whale?

When it's a shark!

The whale shark's mouth is 1.5 metres wide.

A whale shark can grow to 12 metres long.

The gigantic whale shark is one of the biggest fish in the sea.

Whale sharks visit the reef to feed on plankton and tiny fish.

A whale shark slurps in a mouthful of water filled with plankton. It closes its mouth and pushes the water out through its gills. This leaves the shark with a tasty mouthful of food.

From tiny coral polyps to giant sharks, the Great Barrier Reef provides a home and food for many living things.

Big or little, everyone is welcome at the busy reef!

A Coral Reef Food Web

A food web shows who eats who in a habitat.

This food web shows the connections between some of the living things on a coral reef.

Plants and algae can make the food they need for energy inside themselves. To do this, they need sunlight.

Manta ray

Fish

Whale shark

Sea anemone

Sea turtle

Plankton (Tiny animals, plants and algae)

The arrows mean: **eaten by**

Coral

Plants

Glossary

algae
Plant-like living things that mostly grow and live in water. Like plants, algae make their own food using sunlight.

camouflage
Colours, markings or body parts that help an animal blend into its habitat.

coral reef
A large mass of rock, made from the skeletons of tiny animals called coral polyps.

gills
Body parts that some animals, including fish, use for breathing underwater.

habitat
The place where a living thing, such as a plant or animal, makes its home. Coral reefs, forests and deserts are all types of habitats.

mate
To get together to produce young.

mucus
A slimy, protective substance produced by an animal's or person's body.

parasite
A living thing that lives in or inside another living thing.

plankton
Microscopic living things, such as animals and algae, that float in water.

predator
An animal that hunts and eats other animals.

tentacle
A long, thin body part that an animal uses for feeling, grabbing or moving about.

texture
How the surface of something feels, for example, smooth, rough or lumpy.

Index

Learn More Online

To learn more about life on a coral reef, go to
www.rubytuesdaybooks.com/habitats